MULTISITE CHURCH PITFALLS

7 Dangers You Cannot Afford to Ignore

by

David D'Angelo & Ryan Stigile

DEDICATION

To Brooke, Nico, Gino & Mila: may our memories never exceed our dreams. You inspire me to keep going. To my parents: thanks for showing me what faith, leadership and generosity look like in the real world.

-D.D.

To Emily, for your constant encouragement through every pitfall I've encountered. Thanks for leading me to discover the deeper learnings and always pointing me back to God. And to my parents for modeling healthy church leadership well before I ever knew I would need the example.

-R.S.

CONTENTS

ACKNOWLEDGMENTS

There is no way to acknowledge everyone who played a part in the learnings that we write about in this book. We wish we could, but rather than miss someone and not get invited to their wedding, we thought about this section with different perspective. So here are a few things we acknowledge:

We acknowledge that we do not have the multisite church movement figured out.

We acknowledge that sharing what you learn along the way is healthy both for yourself and for those that follow.

We acknowledge that any sincere effort to help the local church pursue health is worthwhile.

We acknowledge that together is always better than apart.

Thanks for reading, we hope you enjoy.

// 1 //

INTRODUCTION: MULTISITE CREATES

MORE PROBLEMS THAN IT SOLVES

Multisite will multiply exactly who you are today. Nothing more. Nothing less.

You and your team have been dreaming about the potential growth that comes through adding new campuses to your church. This isn't selfish dreaming either. Your church has created environments to engage the unchurched, developed a discipleship pathway to help people grow spiritually, and equipped leaders to advance the mission. All of that is worthy of multiplication.

But...there is always a but...

The multiplication of multisite does not discriminate. It is not only the good that grows. Multisite has a way of expanding or reproducing *everything* in your church. What were once tiny cracks in strategy will become gaps in your ministry. Small concerns will expand into large problems. Slight misunderstandings that are easy to overlook will become significant communication breakdowns that halt progress. Unhealthy systems and leaders will become widely exposed.

Going multisite fixes nothing. It only multiplies everything.

Most teams spend more time planning and dreaming for the launch of a campus than they do preparing to *operate* as a multisite church. Imagine if a professional baseball team operated that way. What if they spent their entire offseason planning and dreaming for Opening Day?

> *Most teams spend more time planning and dreaming for the launch of a campus than they do preparing to operate as a multisite church.*

They might have a great marketing campaign, sign one quality starting pitcher, and put together an exciting celebration. But their momentum would end after the first nine innings. The other 161 games would be difficult to attend, creating a miserable season for both the players and the fans.

Unfortunately, many churches are not much different in their multisite initiative. They spend more time planning and dreaming about the campus *launch* than they do preparing for the entire ministry *season*. Before long, they find themselves short on staff, stretched for time, and lacking the systems they need to lead people to next steps. This shortsighted approach impacts every campus, not just new ones. There is no way to contain the damage.

Successful multisite churches do more than launch a new location. They plan ahead to operate as a multisite church, not just function as a church with additional campuses. This is an important distinction with significant consequences.

A well-executed multisite strategy can truly impact an entire region. We've seen it over and over again, in urban, suburban and rural settings. And we want to see God use your church to build His kingdom in your region as well. Truly, we want to help you avoid the pitfalls that we have encountered along the way in our own multisite journey.

The pitfalls in the following chapters describe what we didn't know that we didn't know. These are the learnings that came through both progress and problems. Some of it may even be advice we first ignored. Either way, it is our hope that your church can avoid these pitfalls and launch campuses that have a winning ministry season far beyond their Opening Day.

// 2 //

PITFALL #1: HAVING THE *WHAT*

WITHOUT THE *WHY*

Hidden behind the meetings, the announcements, the search for the right location, and even the hiring of staff for your new campus is *something* that is driving your desire to be multisite. This thing that is creating such hope and excitement for your church can also be one of your most damaging pitfalls.

It's your *why*.

It's the real reason behind this big decision that changes everything about your church. Your *why* is the true motives and purpose for adding new campuses.

Starting out, your purpose is subtle. Its power is not immediately felt. Yes, in the beginning, people will want to know why you are going multisite. But any answer is masked by the shiny excitement of a new community to reach, an innovative ministry risk, new technology, an impressive story to tell, and a big launch with potential for incredible growth. Too often the allure of the new quiets the critical question of *why.*

But it never stays quiet for long. Eventually the newness of a campus launch fades and a normal rhythm begins to set in. Every church leader knows that normal is not easy. As soon as momentum slows, questions emerge. And right in that moment, the power of *why* shows up.

You see, when obstacles arise, when core volunteers step off the team, when momentum wanes, when critics speak out, when finances tighten, when programming excellence drifts, and when technology fails, the foundation your church will turn to is your *why.* And your solution to each challenge will be directly tethered to it.

Our Journey

When we launched headlong into the multisite movement at NewPointe Community Church, we did it for two reasons. First, we deeply believed that everyone spends forever somewhere. We were committed to doing something about that. Second, we believed that the local church had to stay local to stay fully effective.

> *As soon as momentum slows, questions emerge. And right in that moment, the power of why shows up.*

At that point in our church's story, many people were driving more than 40 minutes to our original campus. Yet we knew that those driving beyond 20 minutes were not regularly engaging in their church. They may have attended occasionally on Sundays, but they did not serve, join a small group, or fully involve their kids in ministry environments.

This is why we decided to go multisite. To be effective, our local church had to truly be local.

So why did *you* make the decision to go multisite? Doing the hard work of defining your purpose is a critical step for your leadership team. Here are some idea to help make this hard work make sense:

1. When crafting your *why*, think Twitter not sermon.

Mark Twain once said, "Forgive me for writing such a long letter. I did not have time to write a short one."

Your stated *why* should be more campaign slogan than dissertation. It deserves a great statement that can be repeated and spread quickly because it is so easy to understand. It should be catchy, inspiring, and at the same time paint a picture of a future that everyone wishes they could experience. If it is not any of these, it becomes too easy to lose. Even worse, it can become too easy to forget. Then, in the absence of a reason *why*, people will fill in the blank with whatever is best for them.

Don't settle for a long letter or loose statements about your purpose for going multisite. Take the time to write a short one that people can take with them. Here are three tests for a purpose that will generate momentum:

> **-Clear** - Can someone who is not from your church understand it without any explanation? (Think 1980 Ronald Reagan - "Are you better off than you were four years ago?")

> **-Compelling** - Does it move someone's heart to Kingdom action and selfless behavior? (Think 1928 President Herbert Hoover - "A chicken in every pot. A car in every garage.")

> **-Consistent** - Is it catchy and easy to remember? (Think 1952 President Dwight D. Eisenhower - "I Like Ike")

If you were to ask 10 random people in your church why you were multisite, would they share an answer that is clear, compelling and consistent?

2. What is worth remembering is worth repeating.

In every organization, vision naturally leaks. People have full lives, and anything that does not matter to them personally is quickly forgotten. But that does not mean you should stop trying. It means you must become creatively redundant and relentless in communicating your *why*.

Church leaders have a tendency to think that saying something once is saying it enough. But priorities should never get "once and done" treatment. If you aren't willing to repeat your *why* over and over to your staff, your board, and your congregation, then you are willing to lose your way. Figuring out how to saturate your church with your purpose for multisite is not out of reach for your team. These ideas will help you get started:

-Identify all of the communication channels that are available to your church. Think beyond the weekly announcement, message, and church email to consider everything including volunteer team huddles, social media posts, and community press releases.

-Empower someone other than the lead pastor to wake up every day thinking about how to better communicate your *why*. This person should be given full access to identify and seize opportunities to creatively communicate.

> *If you aren't willing to repeat your why over and over . . . then you are willing to lose your way.*

-Leverage the power of story. It is one thing for a leader to express vision. It is a more credible thing for him or her to share personal stories of life change that took place because you launched a new campus.

Are you communicating a meaningful why over and over again?

3. Use your *why* as a decision-making filter.

Every leader has a decision filter used to process through choices. In a multisite setting, the only way to truly determine if an opportunity is right is for your church is to run it through the filter of your *why*.

When decisions arise, the real question will be this: Are you using the *why* you promoted to make decisions? Or was it just a slogan you used to move people in the direction you wanted?

Think about it this way: If you are truly pursuing multisite to grow your attendance, every opportunity for "more" will be urgently pursued because your attendance defines your success. If you are pursuing multisite to position the local church to reach more communities for Christ, then leadership empowerment, health, and development will define your success. Whenever you face a challenging decision, simply feel stuck, or when are trying to measure success, filter your decisions through your *why*.

Are the decisions you're making in line with the why you're communicating?

So what is the real purpose behind your vision for multisite? Can you communicate it in a single tweet? Can your board members, staff, and congregation repeat it clearly without stumbling for words? Do you leverage it in meetings to make decisions with purpose?

If you're not sure, take time to craft your *why* before you move further toward your vision for multisite. Doing so will bring everyone on the same page so you can truly move forward together.

// 3 //

PITFALL #2: FAILING TO DEFINE

YOUR MULTISITE APPROACH

The decision to go multisite is no doubt a significant one. It is also a very broad decision that can be defined in a number of ways. A congregation and staff can rally around the vision for multisite only to run into a significant pitfall. This happens when people start realizing that "being multisite" can be interpreted to mean a number of different things. Before long, people start asking, "Which multisite approach are we taking?" When everyone answers that question differently, the excitement around your vision is traded for confusion among the players.

If you do not begin to address this pitfall early, you will run into it when it is least convenient. Just imagine the chaos that will come with several campuses, several staff teams, and several congregations operating with different understandings of what it means to be one church.

Few multisite churches experience a problem of *correctness* where issues are caused by the *wrong* strategy. Far more experience a problem of *clarity,* suffering from the lack of a *defined* strategy. Before taking big steps to become a multisite church, you must gather senior leaders to define your multisite approach. As you do, you'll need to include four key variables in the conversation: Teaching, Worship, Discipleship Models, and Organizational DNA.

4 KEY VARIABLES IN YOUR MULTISITE APPROACH

	FRANCHISE APPROACH	LOCALIZED APPROACH	CHURCH PLANT APPROACH
1. Teaching	- Shared Content - Shared Speaker	- Shared Content - Different Speakers	- Different Content - Different Speakers
2. Worship	- Same Music	- Same Style - Different Music	- Different Styles
3. Discipleship Models **(Adults & Family Life)**	- Same Discipleship Models	- Same Core Ministries - Different Secondary Ministries	- Different Discipleship Models
4. Organizational DNA	- Same Mission - Same Global Vision - Same Values	- Same Mission - Different Local Visions - Same Values	- Different Local Missions - Different Local Visions Different Local Values

Key Multisite Variable #1: Teaching

One of the first questions to surface when a church decides to go multisite is, "How are we going to handle the teaching?" This variable comes with the greatest implications on technology and cost. As you begin to address the teaching variable, consider the following three approaches:

Franchise Approach: Shared Content, Shared Speaker

One of the best ways to maintain "one church in multiple locations" is to share the exact same speaker each weekend across campuses. Some multisite churches opt to stream live video teaching to each campus from one central campus. This is how Elevation Church (Charlotte, NC) began into multisite. At NewPointe, streaming costs and the internet bandwidth available in our region led us to pre-record our teaching during the week for video playback at every campus that weekend. However you choose to go about it, sharing the exact same teaching at every campus provides the greatest opportunity to communicate unified vision and values across your campuses. It also further leverages the strong teaching gifts presently on your team.

Localized Approach: Shared Content, Different Speakers

Some multisite churches want to leverage the same teaching content across every campus while simultaneously platforming the spiritual leadership of their campus pastors. To do this, they enable campus pastors to speak live from similar sermon outlines. The biblical texts and principles remain the same while each campus pastor includes his or her own stories and illustrations. Mountain Lake Church provides a great example of this with four locations north of Atlanta. They went as far as to title each local leader the "Campus & Teaching Pastor." Leveraging different speakers with shared content keeps a local voice at every location. At the same time, it adds an extra required skill when evaluating future staff members. Campus pastors must be great communicators in addition to great leaders. It also requires that they spend a significant amount of time each week developing their sermons.

Church Planting Approach: Different Content, Different Speakers

In some situations, lead pastors choose to empower their campus pastors to independently develop their own unique messages. There is little to no desire for congruent teaching across campuses. This requires each campus pastor to invest a significant amount of time in sermon preparation.

Key Multisite Variable #2: Worship

After defining your approach to multisite teaching, it is time to determine how you will program worship and creative arts across multiple locations. Here again, you'll find three unique approaches.

Franchise Approach: Shared Music

At NewPointe, we utilized the exact same service plans and music set lists each weekend at every campus. This allowed us to maximize the time spent arranging music and developing creative moments in worship. Worship leaders at each campus spent much less time developing plans for each Sunday and much more time investing in their volunteers.

Localized Approach: Same Style, Different Music

North Point Ministries led by Andy Stanley chooses to maintain the same music style at every location while giving each campus the freedom to choose their own set lists each weekend. An organization-wide list of songs gives local leaders consistent boundaries while maintaining their freedom to build their own services.

Church Planting Approach: Different Styles

Some multisite churches believe that the approach to worship should be based on the culture in which the campus exists along with the strengths of the worship leader. This may be needed when campus locations are in significantly different cultural areas of a city or region. At North Way Christian Community, campuses are in anything but cookie-cutter locations. Words like urban, suburban, collegiate, city, commuter and close-knit can all be used in some combination to describe each individual campus context. With that, music teams at North Way still choose songs from an established list. But they have the freedom to utilize styles that translate well to their local context. This approach provides a richer local context to worship style when an area requires it.

Key Multisite Variable #3: Discipleship Models (Adults and Family Life)

Many churches go multisite before fully refining their discipleship models, only to find them much more complicated a few years later. The primary challenge in this area is that of scale -- the ability for the same approach to work effectively at campuses of different sizes. In nearly every situation, the original campus operates with more ministries than a smaller campus can handle. In those cases, should the smaller campus get to choose which ministries and programs it wants to adopt? Can it create new ministries that fit its smaller size? These are key questions that must be answered early in the life of a multisite church.

Franchise Approach: Same Discipleship Models

Using the same discipleship model across all campuses creates a consistent experience that reflects your shared mission. It also simplifies communications efforts as the same next steps can be promoted everywhere. Coupled with a shared teaching approach, this enables the teaching team to lead people toward specific next steps as a part of their messages. Identical discipleship models also make the most of ministry leaders' time since curriculum and plans can be developed once and utilized at an infinite number of locations. This equips new campuses to operate with less staff.

There is one hidden challenge with the franchised approach. Because new campuses always start smaller than the original, the franchise approach to discipleship models does require some change at the original campus. To operate on a model that every campus can share regardless of size, the original campus will likely have to eliminate some programs that cannot be replicated elsewhere. There is nothing wrong with that reduction. In fact, most churches suffer from operating too many programs and could benefit from this process of trimming back to do more with less.

Localized Approach: Same Core Ministries, Different Secondary Ministries

Another approach to providing ministries at campuses of different sizes is to establish a shared core and allow local development beyond it. Senior leaders may identify the discipleship components that are key to the mission. These could include small groups, assimilation tracks, annual events, etc. Campuses then have the freedom to establish secondary programs as long as the core is well-established and maintained. Those secondary programs should address specific local needs and ultimately lead people to engage further with core ministries. It is important that campus leaders do not neglect the shared core programs for the sake of local initiatives. Entrepreneurial leaders at campuses may struggle with this.

> *For a church to take on a multisite strategy but maintain different discipleship approaches really suggests multiple churches in multiple locations rather than one church in multiple locations.*

Church Planting Approach: Different Discipleship Models

Whether intentionally or accidentally, some multisite churches begin by enabling campus leaders to develop their own models for discipleship. It can seem like a great idea at first. After all, one could argue that different communities have different spiritual needs that must be met.

If that is the philosophy of discipleship among your senior leadership team, a church planting initiative is likely a better strategy than going multisite. More than music style and message delivery, discipleship is the heartbeat of a church. For a church to take on a multisite strategy but maintain different discipleship approaches really suggests multiple churches in multiple locations rather than one church in multiple locations.

Key Variable #4: Organizational DNA

Nothing is more core to a church than its mission, vision, and values. These components express the true heart of the organization and can be seen in everything a church does. Before going far in conversations about multisite, leadership teams must ensure that these components of organizational DNA are clear to the entire staff and congregation. Consider the following definitions of each:

Mission is the reason your church exists. Everything you do aims to accomplish this purpose. It should be defined and well-articulated in a single statement.

Vision is the next big step in accomplishing your mission. It is the direction you feel God calling you toward in this season of approximately three to eight years. This should be described in three to five sentences often accompanied by a single summary phrase for simplified communication. For many churches, going multisite is their next big vision. Remember, vision is a picture of a preferred future so it should be tangible not philosophical.

Values define what is important to your church as you pursue mission and vision. They form the basis for all decision-making. In moments of decision, the team can refer to your values and be reminded of how to determine what is best. Strive to identify the five to eight values that are truly at the core of your DNA. Churches with more than eight will struggle to live by all of them.

Maintaining the same organizational DNA across campuses is essential to truly remain *one church* in multiple locations. That being said, you might choose from a few very slightly different approaches as you transfer this DNA to new campuses.

Franchise Approach: Same Mission, Same Global Vision, Same Values

In this approach, the organizational DNA is identical across every campus. Local leaders do not develop a separate vision for their individual locations or communities. Instead, they may talk about how the church's vision will impact their area.

Localized Approach: Same Mission, Same Global Vision with Different Local Visions, Same Values

Some multisite churches may allow their campus pastors the opportunity to develop a local vision that is in alignment with the church's global vision. They may identify a major need in their community that they want to address through a major step over time. A localized approach to organizational DNA would allow them to do that. Within this approach, campus pastors should be coached to communicate local visions in ways that tie them to the organizational DNA.

Church Planting Approach: Different Missions, Different Visions, Different Values

When a church opts to give campuses the freedom to develop unique missions, visions, and values, it has set itself up for successful church planting. It is only a matter of time before each location is operating in isolation. This path leads to continual confusion and frustration because core priorities are simply incongruent. Leaders who desire this level of local expression would best serve their purposes through a church planting initiative.

A Thought on Church Planting

As you will find throughout this book, we do not believe the church planting approach is a healthy multisite model. There is absolutely nothing wrong with church planting. But if you're going to do it, see it through all the way. Launch a church planting initiative to begin new churches with independent lead pastors, governance, and financial systems. Doing so will not grow your church but it will grow the Kingdom. If God has called you to plant churches, do not hold back those local congregations by trying to keep them under the umbrella of your church.

Defining and Communicating Your Model with Clarity

Churches that hesitate to address these key variables will find themselves stymied by uncertainty years down the road. Create your own grid with the four key variables along with any other variables relevant to your church. Then define your approach in each area and share it with the team.

If God has called you to plant churches, do not hold back those local congregations by trying to keep them under the umbrella of your church.

Do you find yourself leaning toward a franchise approach? If so, it's time to get very clear on how you do ministry. Thinking a localized approach is a better for your church? Start building the pipeline to ensure you can have great leaders at every campus. Looking at taking a church planting approach? Start having the conversations with your board about starting new organizations. Whichever approach you find yourself taking, communicating it with clarity from the outset equips your entire team to move together in the right direction.

// 4 //

PITFALL #3: UNDERVALUING

THE CAMPUS PASTOR

One of the greatest pitfalls in the multisite movement lies with the Campus Pastor. Leadership sets the tone and pace for any organization. You can have the best strategy, the clearest plan, and the greatest resources, but if you do not identify and invest in the right leader for each campus, you're setting yourself up for frustration and failure.

It is hard to put a number on the value of a campus pastor. But it is certainly greater than his or her salary. Each campus launch is an investment of hundreds of thousands of dollars, not to mention the annual operating expenses that will follow. To undervalue the campus pastor position is poor stewardship of a significant kingdom investment.

> When you don't take the time to hire the right person, you undervalue the position.

> When you don't invest time and money into training, you undervalue the position.

When you don't walk closely with him or her through the campus launch process, you undervalue the position.

And when you don't develop a leadership pipeline for future campus pastors, you undervalue the position and limit your vision for future campuses.

The campus pastor is not a "light" version of a lead pastor or a substitute for an associate pastor. Neither is it simply a stepping stone between youth pastor and church planter. It is a unique role requiring specific gifts to lead within a specific ministry strategy. It is hard to identify the right campus pastors for your team until you have established your *why* and your multisite approach as described in the previous chapters.

> *To undervalue the campus pastor position is poor stewardship of a significant kingdom investment.*

So how can you avoid this pitfall with your campus pastors? It comes down to hiring the right leaders, investing time in their development, and empowering them to use their gifts.

Hire campus pastors with three critical qualities

The campus pastor position is a unique ministry role requiring unique gifts. While your needs may vary depending on your strategy and location, there are three universally transferrable qualities that every campus pastor should exhibit to be successful.

1. High Relational Connector

Campus pastors serve as the primary ambassador for your church in their communities. The ability to connect with local leaders in government, business, and education is essential. Your campus pastors must be able to walk into a room and quickly connect with people they have never met. Otherwise, you'll never have the opportunity for influence and impact in the community that comes with being a true member of it.When hiring, ask, "Could I see him/her connecting with anyone from anywhere?" High relational connectors are enjoyable to be around and can raise the positive energy in any setting.

2. Proven Team Builder

The need for strong, passionate volunteers is no greater than during the launch of a campus. With that, the ability to cast vision and recruit people is paramount. Campus pastors must also be able to quickly identify leaders, develop them within the church's DNA, and empower them to lead teams. Successful campus pastors know how to develop leadership structures to mobilize multiple teams across the ministries of a campus.

When hiring, ask, "Does he/she have a proven track record of building multiple ministry teams through leaders?" Remember that past history is the best predictor of future performance.

3. Strong Executing Leader

Within most multisite strategies, the ability to "get things done" is paramount to the role of campus pastor. While campus pastors should contribute perspective in conversations about ministry strategies, they do not have to be highly creative or the inventor of plans. They do, however, need to be strong implementers of plans through people. Too often, we undervalue the ability to execute in leadership. Without it, the greatest ideas never become reality. In your case, you need ideas to become reality in multiple locations. That is not possible without campus pastors who can execute.

In their book *Execution*, Larry Bossidy (CEO, Honeywell) and Ram Charan (business advisor) make the case that, "Organizations don't execute unless the right people, individually and collectively, focus on the right details at the right time." At each campus, this focus on the right details begins with the Campus Pastor.

When hiring, ask, "Will he/she be fulfilled by implementing our strategies? Or will there be a desire to reinvent them at the campus?"

Hiring great campus pastors is no easy task. We believe that the ideal approach is to develop future campus pastor from within your existing team. Be patient until you've found the leader who exhibits these three essential qualities. Remember, you're selecting someone to steward a significant kingdom investment.

Ask new campus pastors to "do nothing"

In order to truly become one church in multiple locations, each campus pastor must capture and reflect the DNA of your ministry. They must understand, embody, and reflect the following elements from their core:

-Your mission
-Your vision
-Your values
-Your culture
-Your ministry strategies
-Your operating systems

This is different from the typical new hire. Most new hires walk into an existing culture and learn the DNA from their team over time. A new campus pastor is not being invited to simply join a culture, he or she is being charged with replicating a culture. Replication is impossible without full understanding.

The only way to develop that level of understanding is through time and proximity. New campus pastors must spend their early days focused on three priorities:

1. Having development and training conversations about the organization's DNA
2. Developing relationships with central or "sending campus" leaders who they will soon be working with from a distance
3. Shadowing an existing campus pastor throughout the week (or the lead pastor if this is your first campus launch)

Most of the other people on your team will not see tangible results from those three priorities. To them, it may look like the new campus pastor was hired early to simply "do nothing." In reality, the work being done is on the inside of the person as he or she comes to understand and reflect your culture from the core. The tangible results will be seen once the campus launches and truly exists as a full representation of your organization's mission in a new location.

Skipping a thorough on-ramping process is a pitfall that undercuts the potential growth and health of a new campus launch. So how long does this take? If you're hiring a campus pastor from outside the organization, we recommend you do so 12 months prior to launch. It truly takes that amount of time to help someone become a full carrier of your DNA. That onboarding time could be less for an existing staff member you are developing internally.

Skipping a thorough on-ramping process is a pitfall that undercuts the potential growth and health of a new campus launch.

Empower campus pastors to champion and advocate

Campus pastors sit in one of the most difficult leadership roles within an organization. They regularly get pulled in two directions. On one side, they have the expectations of a central leadership team developing organizational ministry strategies. (We'll talk more about that team in the next chapter.) On the other side, they have a local campus with specific strengths and weaknesses along with a local community with unique opportunities and needs. Managing that tension is no simple task.

The only way to lead through this tension is to *champion* and *advocate*. Campus pastors must be able to champion the mission, vision, and values of your church within their community. At the same time, they must have the opportunity to advocate for their campuses' needs with central leaders. They require a seat at the table when ministry strategies are being developed and evaluated.

When you train campus pastors to both champion the vision at their campus and advocate for the needs of their campus, you empower them to manage the tension that is required to truly exist as one church in multiple locations.

You cannot put a price tag on your campus pastors. There is never a point at which you've invested in them *enough*. Take as much time as you need to hire the right leaders, develop them in your culture, and empower them to manage the tension that comes with being multisite. In doing so, you'll see an incredible return as they leverage your resources to lead another community closer to Jesus.

// 5 //

PITFALL #4: LEAVING CAMPUS LEADERS WITHOUT

CENTRALIZED SUPPORT

When launching a multisite strategy, one of the earliest questions is, "How will we replicate our worship service with excellence?" It makes sense that this is a top concern given that it is the largest and most visible component of a church. However, being one church in multiple locations is a much deeper endeavor than the duplication of a worship service.

Think about all of the things that make your church unique and meaningful to the people who walk through its doors each weekend. These include your children's environments, student ministry, small groups, Bible studies, volunteer teams, recovery groups, and likely more. Each ministry area that is core to your mission must be replicated successfully at new campuses at the same level of effectiveness in which they originally existed. It is easy to assume that campuses will naturally absorb and replicate what is most important. After all, the leaders have seen the programs in place at your original campus and they can always ask questions as they go.

That assumption is a significant pitfall that will inhibit a new campus' ability to fully impact its community. Here are a few reasons replicating a ministry at a new campus is not so simple:

1. Your ministry strategies are more detailed and refined than most think.

If you're a multisite church, or even considering the strategy, you didn't get to this point by accident. You've been using intentional strategies to reach people and lead them toward spiritual next steps. Those approaches involve a number of details and nuances, most of which live in the minds of one or two leaders in each area. It is more than new campus leaders could pick up in a few conversations. They may not even know the right questions to ask.

2. Your ministry strategies will continue developing over time.

You didn't build a team to sit back and manage programs. You recruited leaders who would never stop building and growing the ministry. Your church will undoubtedly continue refining its strategies over time. As it does, it will be difficult for campuses to keep up with and leverage these improvements.

3. Ministry vision continually leaks.

This is not a foreign concept for church leaders. But it does become more complex when you go multisite. At one location, you are readily available to plug and patch vision leaks for your team. But how will your campus leaders at multiple sites be reminded of the purpose behind all of their efforts? If there isn't a plan for this, your *why* will be lost.

Replicating Ministry at New Campuses

So how can you ensure that you truly exist as one church in multiple locations through every aspect that makes your church unique? Start by asking this driving question for each ministry area: *"Who wakes up every day thinking about this for all campuses?"*

For example, who spends each day thinking about the quality of small groups in every community you exist in? It is easy to say, "We've been doing small groups for years. Everyone already knows how to create them." If that is your answer, you are denying the real needs of those who lead ministries at campuses.

When a church goes multisite without clearly defining a central leader for each ministry area, it is setup to experience a number of challenges:

Each area of ministry needs a single individual taking responsibility for development and communication throughout your campuses. These leaders must be responsible for ministry results, clarifying and championing ministry DNA, and resourcing the local leaders at campuses. Resourcing should come in several forms including ministry plans, systems, and personal coaching. When a church goes multisite without clearly defining a central leader for each ministry area, it is setup to experience a number of challenges:

-Critical meetings for evaluation and ministry growth do not happen
-Invaluable feedback from newer campuses is not heard
-Communication of critical information within each ministry area does not take place
-Strategic development does not happen across campuses
-Campus ministry leaders never experience personal coaching related to their roles
-Vision leaks at each campus and even drifts in new directions that are difficult to correct

Where might you need central leaders? Below are the key areas to start with:

1. **Creative Arts:** service planning, production, and worship

2. **Family Ministry:** children's ministry, student ministry, and parenting resources
3. **Adult Discipleship:** next steps, small groups, leadership development
4. **Volunteer Connections:** recruitment, connection systems, team culture
5. **Communications:** branding, promotions, marketing, website, print material
6. **Finance:** budgets, financial systems, purchase orders, reimbursements
7. **IT/IS:** technology, church database, infrastructure

It is important to note that these essential roles are typically considered "dotted line" relationships on the organizational chart. They don't supervise or provide point leadership to team members across campuses. That is the role of campus pastors. Instead central leaders take responsibility for the ongoing strategic development of their specific ministry areas.

How Do We Afford All This Staff?

By now you may be thinking, "Won't all these ministry area leaders be expensive? We can't afford all the additional hires right now!" That is perfectly understandable and truly unnecessary if you are just beginning your multisite strategy. Starting out, it is most important to define who has ultimate responsibility for results and resourcing in each area, even if that "central leader" also serves at a campus.

Below are a few way to introduce central ministry leadership in you structure:

2-3 Total Campuses: Lead from the Sending Campus

When initially launching into multisite, your original campus can serve as the "sending campus" to lead one or two others. Ministry leaders at the sending campus are also responsible for setting the other campuses up to win. They should regularly ask the following questions as they lead:

> -Will this ministry plan work effectively at a smaller campus, potentially in a portable environment?
>
> -Am I addressing the needs of newer campuses with a younger, smaller team?
>
> -In what ways do my counterpart leaders at other campuses need to grow and develop? How can I invest directly into them?

These main campus leaders should hold team meetings involving all campuses at least bi-weekly. They should also meet individually with the leaders of other campuses for personal development at least once a month.

2-3 Total Campuses: Lead Influencers at Various Campuses

An alternative to driving everything from the sending campus is to establish a "lead influencer" for each ministry area. These influencers can be working at any individual campus and also take the lead for their ministry across the entire organization. This enables you to resource your newest campuses with some of your strongest leaders to help them get off the ground.

4 Total Campuses: Central Ministry Team

By the time you reach four total campuses, it is important to be establishing a centralized leadership team. These ministry leaders no longer work for a specific campus but instead take responsibility for resourcing all campuses with strategies and ministry plans. They also continue coaching campus leaders in their areas. This sets you up with a structure that can truly scale as the organization continues to grow.

As you navigate each transition in the structure of your leadership, it is important to communicate with your team in detail and well in advance. Some long-time ministry leaders may not be given a central leadership position. This can feel like a loss of influence as others around them gain an equal or stronger voice in their ministry. These feelings are natural, understandable, and cannot be ignored. Lead everyone with high levels of availability and care, helping them identify how they are wired to contribute significantly to the mission of your growing organization.

// 6 //

PITFALL #5: LACKING A FRAMEWORK

FOR DECISION-MAKING

"Who makes this call?"

You've heard this muttered, implied or outright voiced in meetings when an outstanding issue still needed to be resolved. If you already exist as a multisite church, it has likely come up regarding a number of issues such as worship service plans, event schedules, curriculum adjustments, and so on. But the specific question asked is not always the point. The real issue is the lack of a clear decision-making framework that helps healthily navigate these tensions and remain unified as a multisite church. Delaying a decision for the sake of team unity will only last so long. Eventually individuals must be empowered to lead forward.

When a multisite team lacks a decision-making framework, it defaults to the lead pastor in every moment of disagreement. This overwhelms his or her calendar with countless conversations. Additionally, though he or she may provide a clear decision, everyone still walks away frustrated. Some are displeased by the decision itself. Others are frustrated by the process of decision-making. The lead pastor wonders why no one else on his or her team seems capable of leading.

Why You Need a Decision-Making Framework

Most churches mistake an organizational chart for a decision-making framework. While established hierarchies can keep many issues at bay with timely decisions, multisite still provides a different level of complexity. Ministry staff often find themselves looking to both a campus pastor and a central ministry leader for direction. This challenges staff members to work both *up* and *across* the organization. When you clarify who makes which calls, the following indicators of team health are likely to improve:

When a multisite team lacks a decision-making framework, it defaults to the lead pastor in every moment of disagreement.

1. Leadership Development

Decision-making is a part of developing as a leader. When only a select few make decisions of consequence, only a select few are fully developing. Creating boundaries that enable leaders to make decisions allows them ownership of their role and a chance to gain experience through both successes and mistakes.

2. Team Culture

When leaders are empowered, and know their boundaries of influence, the culture of the team improves. People stop acting politically and start focusing on empowering other leaders. Volunteer teams also feel the difference between an empowered staff and a controlled staff because the trickle-down effect is unavoidable.

3. Team Focus

Avoiding the constant team-wide pit stop to address the question of "who makes the call?" allows a team to run further and stall out less. It also frees everyone up to remain focused on ministry development.

4. Problem-Solving

Creating a framework for critical decisions enables a team to more quickly identify system breakdowns and vision leaks. As you'll see through the framework we provide, when a team has the language to identify the type of problem they are experiencing, they can more quickly develop a solution. The shared language that a decision-making framework provides will set your team up to communicate better when addressing issues.

Decision-making is a part of developing as a leader. When only a select few make decisions of consequence, only a select few are fully developing.

An Actual Model

Because the concept of a decision-making framework may seem foreign at first, we're providing the one we developed in our own multisite experience. To begin, we identify the four universally consistent components of every ministry:

1. **Ministry Mission:** The primary intent. This is the core *why* behind a specific ministry.
2. **Ministry Strategies & Resources:** The major programs and plans within a ministry along with the tools to implement those plans.
3. **Ministry Application:** The detailed execution of Ministry Strategies and Resources that are implemented at each individual campus. This is where unique community context is expressed.
4. **Ministry People:** The ground-level volunteer team that is recruited, developed, trained and retained.

Along with these ministry components, we identify the key stakeholders involved in making decisions. Consider the following three:

1. **Senior Leadership Team:** This the senior-most staff leadership team within the organization.
2. **Central Ministry Leaders:** This team resources and supports ministry for all campuses from a centralized position. Typically this group includes staff members who visit all campuses often.
3. **Campus Ministry Leaders:** This is the team of staff who work at individual campuses, including campus pastors.

With these areas defined, we clarify which leaders have the authority to lead in moments of decision regarding each of the four components of ministry. Additionally, we clarify which leaders should truly have the opportunity to influence an area of decision-making. While those with influence may not make the final call, they should have a real opportunity to share their insights and experiences.

The following chart illustrates how decisions are made regarding each of the four ministry components.

	Ministry Mission	Ministry Strategies & Resources	Ministry Application	Ministry People
Campus Leaders		*Influences*	**Leads**	**Leads**
Central Leadership Team	*Influences*	**Leads**	*Influences*	*Influences*
Senior Leadership Team	**Leads**			

Implementing Your Framework

Is it time for you to develop your own decision-making framework? You might start by filling in the decisions that fall within each of the boxes above. Or you might feel the need to build a new framework for your specific multisite approach. In either case, consider the following best practices as you clarify decision-making:

>-Print your framework and have a physical copy to reference in meetings.

>-Leverage the specific language you choose to create synergy and efficiency for your team.

>-Avoid top down vetoes at all cost. The moment your decision-making framework is trumped by senior leaders, it will become discarded by the team.

More often than not, churches do not struggle to give responsibility away. Rather, they fail to give authority that matches the responsibility they transfer. Have the right conversations, define your specific ministry components, and identify which leaders have the authority to make which decisions. Otherwise, your multisite church will constantly be stalled by the question, "Who makes this call?"

// 7 //

PITFALL #6: OPERATING WITHOUT

CRITICAL SYSTEMS

If you've ever boarded a plane, traveled through the air, and landed safely at your destination, you've experienced the power of something that is so easily taken for granted, if not forgotten:

You experienced the power of a checklist.

Pilots, with all of their extensive training and experience, leverage the routine, systematic power of a checklist. Taking off is a repeatable system that is broken down into detailed steps. The same is true of landing. They fly with more than just a future destination they hope to reach. They have clear systems to ensure they get there.

Every airplane passenger, knowingly or not, benefits from the fact that someone took the time to think through *and* write down the systematic process of flying. They are thankful that the airline had a plan to operate that flight, rather than winging it from memory. Every person who attends the campuses of your church deserves the same experience.

Visions Need Systems

Dreaming about the future often comes very natural to church staff teams. After a few meetings together and some shared language, everyone can begin to picture the future destination together. Vision is necessary in multisite ministry. But equally important to vision is the detailed planning and "checklisting" of how the team will reach its desired destination.

Without systems, visions perish.

Systems and Multisite

Every ministry team that is up and running already has some level of systematic approach to ministry. Failing to capture those approaches and relay them to new campuses will set them up for organizational chaos. In *Checklist Manifesto*, Atul Gawande explains that human failure within organizations is a result of two factors. The first is *ignorance*; not knowing what you don't know. The second is *ineptitude*; the inconsistent or incorrect application of knowledge.

> ## *Without systems, visions perish.*

If your campus pastor is constantly having to re-develop systems that are already in place at your first campus, he or she is spending precious time exerting sideways energy. The same is true for every campus ministry leader. This hinders real progress toward the vision and causes everyone to feel stuck.

Consider the following benefits that clearly developed systems can bring to your church and team:

-Systems allow for multiplication of leadership because more people can know what others already know.

-Systems create mental margin for leaders, allowing them to focus on critical priorities.

-Systems help leaders determine if a breakdown in ministry is the result of leadership or a system in need of change.

-Systems handle repetitive processes that are critical to the functioning of your church.

Taking time to establish specific systems is a worthwhile investment. It avoids the clumsy (and preventable) pitfall of an unsystematic approach to ministry.

Four Critical Systems

As you begin your ministry journey, gather the team to think about these four types of systems you will need in place:

1. Critical Information Flow

Your campuses need an incoming and outgoing system of delivery for physical products. Think of this like an inbox and outbox for curriculum, guest connection cards, offerings, new literature, bulletins, mail, etc. Having this in place helps you avoid moments of, "I thought you were picking up this week's kids curriculum. I guess we'll have to wing it." With a good system, winging it should never be required.

2. Communication Priority

When it comes to church communications, everyone feels like their message is priority. With more campuses, that pressure for priority will feel even greater. Your ministries may have global events, local events, and even dual-campus events to promote. But there is only so much that can be communicated through stage announcements, bulletins, and the website. Develop a system to determine what gets promoted and where. Otherwise, different leaders will define it for themselves.

> *When it comes to church communications, everyone feels like their message is priority.*

Disunity and misalignment are sure to result if you do not give this attention.

3. Feedback Loops

In a multisite environment, feedback (code word for "opinions") flows down from the top quite well. Central ministry leaders will get good at helping newer campuses identify ways to improve. But how do campus leaders return that favor? How can ministry teams help explain what does and does not work with the ministry plans they receive? If feedback is only flowing one direction, it will be quickly disregarded by campuses as useless noise or damaging criticism. The word *loop* is key to this system. Feedback needs to flow both to and from campus and central leaders. It is important for your communication and meeting structures to reflect this.

4. New Guest Connections

This system helps close the backdoor to your church. When a guest visits a campus and provides personal information via child check-in, connection cards, or giving, is there a specific plan to follow-up and help them get connected? Is that plan repeatable at all of your campuses? Do not leave this to each individual team to figure out. It's too valuable. The hot iron of a visiting guest cools quickly. Take time to set the exact process to follow, from automatic emails to next steps for guests. Your team and your guests will appreciate you for it.

When it comes to repeatable systems, these four types are just the starting point of what needs to be established. Each one should be written down and given an owner to regularly monitor it for continued effectiveness. If it is not written, it is only a suggestion.

To help you think further about the multisite systems your church needs, here is a list of starter questions for which you should have an answer:

-Who counts attendance and where/how do they report it?

-How does the message video get delivered?

-How do you handle the offering, from the moment it is received to the moment it is deposited in the bank?

-How does a campus promote its events online (website, social media, email, etc.)?

-What happens when technology fails during a message video (both kids and adults)?

-How do you communicate weather closings?

-What will/won't we promote on our website?

-What is the timeline and plan for rolling out the full set of ministries at a new campus?

-If you have a creative element that one campus cannot pull off, what is their "Plan B?"

-Is there a planning calendar that creates clear boundaries of non-negotiable and negotiable ministry events? How is it managed?

Take a look through this list and see what it sparks for your team. Then make a list of what systems are in place, which need to be refined, and what needs to be developed. Then go to work creating the systems your campuses need to thrive. Thinking through them will prepare you to better operate as a fully developed multisite ministry, not just a church that launches new locations.

// 8 //

PITFALL #7: CHASING A DREAM INSTEAD OF

LAUNCHING WITH A PLAN

One of the most common mistakes multisite leaders make is underestimating the *requirements* of a campus launch. They have a great vision for the new campus. In their minds, it doesn't look that much different from their existing location. Yet they fail to remember how their current location came into existence. Years of hard work, team building, large financial investments, real estate development, equipment purchasing, and significant moves of God got them to where they are today. Many of those components took a significant amount of time along with the expertise of people outside of the staff.

How could launching a new location be any different?

Unfortunately, many church leaders never move beyond the dream to establish a real plan. Their hearts are dedicated to the vision but their minds have not worked to direct their hands. When they fall into this pitfall, a number of problems arise:

-Volunteer teams are too small and stretched too thin.

-Equipment comes in at the last minute and is not easy to transport

-The appearance of environments at the campus is much less engaging than desired.

-Marketing is delayed because you don't have a venue.

-The team is forced into "crunch mode" at the end, stealing the passion and excitement they once had for the launch.

Unfortunately, many church leaders never move beyond the dream to establish a real plan.

If you do not take steps to establish a clear launch plan, you'll find yourself disappointed by unmet expectations. In this chapter, we walk through some key components to include in your plan in order to avoid this pitfall. Only you and your team can design the details that are best for your church. Here you'll find a framework that can serve as a foundation to your plan.

When You're Ready to Launch

The decision to launch another campus is a critical one. It can either capitalize on momentum or stretch your team and resources too thin to survive. It is not uncommon for visionary leaders to ignore warning signs and press forward to the goal.

Remember the NASA Challenger tragedy? The shuttle used a piece of equipment that had never been tested in temperatures as cold as that day's. The leadership team knew this. Yet they pressed forward with a desire to quickly accomplish the vision. If you ignore the real indicators that reveal when you are and are not ready to launch, you could easily lead your own team to disaster. Here are two indicators that you need to value greatly:

Indicator #1: Your Current Location Is At Capacity

Trying to launch a new location without fully maximizing your current location is a poor stewardship of resources. It sets you up for a weak financial position with little margin at multiple sites. If you haven't fully optimized at least three weekend services at your current location, you're not ready to launch another one. You might say, "We're not at three services but we have the money to launch another campus right now." What impact could that money make if you reinvested it in your current location? How could you use it to reach more people there? If you're already a multisite church, wait until one campus is fully optimized and then launch another out of it.

Indicator #2: Many People Are Driving From A Nearby Community

The best place to launch your next campus is in a community that you have already begun reaching. Your next location will present itself when a significant number of people are driving from it to an existing campus. Some leaders may be tempted to start "missionary campuses" by asking a group of volunteers to help launch a campus in a community where they do not live. That strategy is both expensive and slow-going. It is hard to reach a community where you have no relationships.

Building the Core Team

The core team is by far the most important aspect of your campus launch. Without a committed group of local volunteers, there is no one to utilize your equipment or invite people to attend. Building the core team is the most time consuming component. It can also be the most rewarding as you witness individuals using their gifts to serve in ways they've never done before. Below are several steps to help you establish this team.

1. Vision Meetings

Once you've designated a location for your next campus launch, it is time to start casting vision for it. Hold broad, vision meetings in which you share the heart behind the launch, a basic overview of the plan, and an estimated launch month - likely about one year in the future. Start by holding these meetings at your current location or existing campus closest to the launch location. Next, hold these meetings in the community where you'll be launching. Next Level Church (New England) promotes these vision meetings to the community through yard signs and billboards. It is a great way to invite local individuals who are disengaged by church and share your vision.

2. Campus Pastor Follow-Up

Once you've hosted vision meetings, the real work of the campus pastor begins. This person should follow up personally with everyone who attended. Through emails and phone calls, they can offer to meet with as many individuals or couples as possible. In those one-on-one conversations, the campus pastor should care for the individuals and ask them to prayerfully consider being a part of the launch. It is critical that the campus pastor puts the people before the vision. Vision attracts people to the launch. But most volunteers will join the team because they trust the campus pastor and feel that he or she has their best interests in mind.

3. Leadership Development

As soon as possible, your campus pastor should identify and invest in potential leaders on the team. Do this through regular one-on-one conversations as well as group studies. At NewPointe, we utilized *Deep & Wide* by Andy Stanley to help our leaders further understand our desire to reach unchurched people. You may utilize another resource. But it is important to value potential leaders early by giving them your time and investing in their growth.

4. Community Development

More than anything else, the relationships core team members form with one another will keep them committed through the most trying seasons of the launch. You can never start forging these relationships too soon. Start with monthly core team meetings in the community. There your campus pastor can cast vision, provide trainings, and create an environment for people to connect. As you get closer to the launch, you may want to increase these meetings to every other week.

Launching local small groups in the community prior to the launch also creates a great opportunity for core team community. Additionally, you'll have groups ready for new people to connect with after your launch.

5. Team Organization

As you get 4-6 months out from the launch, you'll be ready to formally organize your core team into specific volunteer teams. Start by recruiting the leaders you've been developing to specific roles. Next, ask core team members to select one or two teams on which they'd be interested in serving. Once you've taken a look at how people have self-selected their teams, you may need to personally ask some to consider a different serving opportunity in which you need more people. In a launch process, volunteers tend to be more flexible with their roles, willing to invest where they can make the greatest difference. Finally, host individual team trainings at one of your existing campuses.

Along the way, be sure to constantly care for your team. Social outings, fun events, along with times of spiritual development and prayer are easy ways to show them that their growth is more important than the growth of your campus. If you truly value the people God has entrusted you with, they will commit themselves to do all they can to reach more people through the campus.

It is one thing to open a campus in a community. It is an entirely different thing to become a member of that community.

Connecting With the Community

It is one thing to open a campus in a community. It is an entirely different thing to become a member of that community. "If you build it, they will come," is never an effective strategy - unless you are Kevin Costner in *Field of Dreams*. While you are in the process of building a team you must also be building relationships with the people you are working to reach. Particularly, there are three groups on which to focus:

1. Connecting With Community Leaders

Establishing relationships with key influencers in the community you are reaching can open opportunities you would never expect. It is amazing how God works through other people when we put ourselves in proximity to them. In our experience, campus venues and key marketing relationships have opened up specifically because of relationships with community leaders.

As soon as possible, reach out to local government officials, school superintendents, county board members, and others. If you aren't sure who to connect with, ask. Members of your core team will likely know many of them and be glad to make an introduction. Investing in these relationships early in the launch process can become incredibly valuable later on when unexpected problems arise.

2. Connect With Local Stakeholders

A local stakeholder is anyone in the community who may be impacted by the decisions of your campus. This includes the managers and schedulers of any rental venues you are considering, leaders of local non-profits you might partner with, and other church leaders in the area. As your campus launch progresses, relationships with members of each of those groups will prove themselves valuable. When one of our NewPointe campus launches ran into scheduling issues with a local high school we were renting, the relationships that had been previously established paved the way to a critical agreement.

By the time you are in a position to need relational capital, it is always too late to try to establish it. You must begin investing in community leaders and local stakeholders well before you even know if you'll need to ask anything of them. When you meet with people, be sure to do three things. Start by valuing the mission of their organization and role. Find out what they truly care about.

Next, share your desire to make a positive difference in the community through your campus. Help them see how your church's involvement there will contribute to their mission. Finally, value the relationship. Buying lunch, sending small gifts, and writing thank you notes all let them know that you truly appreciate them.

3. Connect With the People You are Reaching

The people you are reaching are by far the most important to connect with. They can also be the most difficult. You cannot identify them in a crowd or find their contact information on a website. You can, however, leverage existing relationships and communicate a compelling message.

Encouraging core team members to invite their friends and family members is the number one way to connect with the people you are reaching. This is why it is so important to build a core team with people who live in the area. Remember, the larger the core team, the more connections and personal invitations you'll be able to make throughout the community. The second best way to connect with people is through an effective marketing strategy.

There is no one-size-fits-all approach to marketing. Its effectiveness is largely determined by the demographic of your community, population density, marketing channels available, and the cost of those channels. In our experience, marketing in smaller towns is both less expensive and more effective than trying to "make a splash" in more crowded suburbs and cities.

The best first step in developing your marketing strategy is to meet with local business owners with experience advertising in the area. They will be able to give you an idea of which methods work best. When it comes to the actual design and writing of marketing material, setting a standard of high quality is extremely important. These should be the best looking and most intentional pieces you have ever put together. If you're unsure about the capacity of your internal team, hire this out to a professional firm you trust.

Establishing the Venue

When it comes down to it, you can drop the ball in a lot of areas of your campus launch. But you simply cannot launch a campus without a venue. It is no wonder, then, that establishing it is typically the most stressful part of the process. From dealing with rental contracts to purchasing equipment, your success in this area comes down to your project management abilities. If that is not your area of strength, quickly recruit someone else on your team to oversee this.

1. Purchasing Equipment

Try to envision all of the equipment that exists within your current church building. Think about everything from the lights on the stage to the scissors in your children's environments. Now try to envision shoving all of that equipment into one or two trailers. If your new campus will be portable, you will have to find a way to do just that. If you'll be in a permanent building, you still have a lot of equipment to purchase and install.

Early in the launch process, put together an equipment task force involving someone from each area of ministry familiar with the equipment they use. Often, administrative assistants are more gifted than pastors for this role. Begin making purchase lists and budgets for each area. Identify the shipping times required for the equipment. Then, schedule your ordering accordingly.

If you're going to be a portable campus, designate one individual to oversee the transportation system. He or she should be familiar with the design of trailer layouts and road cases -- most likely someone in your production department. If there is no one on your team capable of this, hire a portable church consultant. If you do not make the investment on the front end, your volunteer team will pay for it every weekend. You cannot afford to make their setup process more difficult than it has to be.

2. Finding Your Venue

As you research potential venues for your campus, keep in mind these critical features:

A. Drive-To Location

It is important to place your campus in a location that people regularly "drive *to*" rather than "drive *from*." The area will likely involve shops and restaurants that people typically frequent. Doing so makes your campus much more visible. It also eliminates the barrier of trying to navigate a new place. At NewPointe, our Canton campus was originally launched in the neighboring town of Louisville, OH. Louisville is a "drive *from*" location primarily made up of commuter families. When we moved the campus to the heart of the shopping district in Canton, attendance immediately began to rise.

We've all heard the phrase, "Location. Location. Location." It's true. This one aspect is more important than any other quality of your venue.

> *It is important to place your campus in a location that people regularly "drive to" rather than "drive from."*

B. Size of Auditorium

It is important to be realistic about the size of auditorium you need. You can expect to launch with an estimated 2x the number of people on your core team. Your opening service may be larger. If you launch in an auditorium that will require two services quickly, be sure to structure your volunteer teams accordingly.

C. Proximity of Children's Space

It is uncomfortable enough for new parents to leave their children in the care of people they have never before met. Even more uncomfortable is leaving them in a room far away from the auditorium. Help families feel safe by keeping children's space as near to the auditorium as possible. Don't undervalue the role this will play in the minds of parents.

D. Sense of Cleanliness

While your venue does not need to be new, it does need to be in good condition. Ensure that the facility will be cleaned before each weekend and that its equipment will be well-maintained. These are items worth noting when negotiating a rental contract.

Launching a campus is one of the largest, most intricate, projects your church will ever manage. It involves nearly every department, requires countless conversations within the community, and will *always* come with unexpected challenges and opportunities. Only you and your team can craft a detailed plan that will work for you. Share this chapter with them and spend a day identifying what will be required and who will own each step. When you arrive at your launch, you will be glad you mapped out the journey before you began.

// 9 //

CONCLUSION: PAVING THE WAY

After considering these major pitfalls, you might be wondering, "Is all the effort to be multisite really worth it?" We speak from experience when we say, "Absolutely." A well-developed multisite church is positioned to lead more people in more places into a relationship with Jesus. It can even do so more quickly with less resources than single-site churches. Unfortunately, many of the stories we hear do not live up to that potential.

In our conversations with multisite church leaders, we encounter far more who are stuck in a pitfall than not. It isn't because they went multisite without a vision. They had inspired many to passionately join them in a new movement. It's because they launched into multisite before they were ready.

Most churches have a vision for multisite that far outpaces their strategy. That sets them up to run fast and hard...right into a pitfall. The good news is this: any pitfall can be avoided when it is prepared for. The question is, will you have the *patience to prepare*?

Spend some time with your leadership team discussing this topic. Put the seven pitfalls on a whiteboard and ask the following questions:

-How would you rate our church in each of these areas?

-Which pitfalls are we most likely to fall into?

-What steps need to be taken today to ensure we avoid key pitfalls in the future?

-How will we be sure our strategy is just as developed as our vision?

If you have questions about how to prepare for multisite - or even how to address pitfalls you're already experiencing as a multisite church - we serve with a great team at *The Unstuck Group* who would love to help.

> *Most churches have a vision for multisite that far outpaces their strategy.*

With a new understanding of your potential pitfalls along with clear plans to avoid them, you'll be set up to make an incredible impact in the communities you're reaching. We're excited to see how God leads you to further His Kingdom through new campuses. If He's given you a vision for multisite, there is no doubt He will continue equipping you to lead forward. Take time to prepare in advance and avoid the pitfalls. As you do, you'll pave the way for more people in more places to experience life change through Jesus.

ABOUT THE AUTHORS

David D'Angelo

For 10 years, Dave served on the Leadership Team at NewPointe Community Church (NE Ohio), serving in multiple roles including Executive Pastor, Campus Pastor, and overseeing the multisite expansion effort that grew from one to six campuses. Now on the staff team at North Way Christian Community (Pittsburgh, PA), Dave leads the Family Matters teams at 5 locations. Dave is passionate about seeing the local church be as effective as possible.

Ryan Stigile

Ryan is the Director of Strategic Resources for The Unstuck Group. Previously, as Director of Expansion at NewPointe Community Church (NE Ohio), Ryan led the launch and development of new multisite campuses. With Mount Paran Church (Atlanta, GA), he guided the leadership team through a strategic change initiative to simplify and align its ministries. Ryan has a Master of Business Administration from Kennesaw State University and degrees in business administration and discipleship ministry from Lee University. He and his wife, Emily, reside in Canton, OH.

46057221R00035

Made in the USA
San Bernardino, CA
03 August 2019